Scripture text
All Scripture quotations in this publication are taken from the Holy Bible,
New International Version (copyright 1973, 1978, 1984, International Bible Society).

Additional text
Melanie Jongsma, © Copyright 1991 by the Bible League. Revised edition © 2003.

Special thanks to
Carl Afman, David Beelen, Marvin and Thelma Hoogland, Nancy Knol, Edward Meyer,
and Janice Willbrandt for their advice and insights.

Published by
Bible League

P.O. Box 28000, Chicago, IL 60628, USA
www.BibleLeague.org
800-871-5445

This resource is also available from these international Bible League office locations:
P.O. Box 4071, Werrington, NSW 2747, Australia (1800-800-937)
P.O. Box 5037, Burlington, Ontario, L7R 3Y8, Canada (800-363-9673)
P.O. Box 77047, Mt. Albert, Auckland 1030, New Zealand (+9-846-5111)

Printed in USA   A100–0051

Your darkest hour

You've gone through other trials.
You've known already that life is not fair.
An endless job search, a ragged divorce—
these things rattled you,
but left your faith intact.
                         Perhaps they even strengthened it-
                clouds often serve as striking backgrour
                                for God's shining lov

But this is a time so dark
it seems to swallow light.
This is a measure so heavy
it crushes your will and smothers your hope.

You are facing possible death.

The reality of it has numbed you,
and you cannot see God or feel His presence.
You've never felt so alone.

But even now
when you are swirling in confusion
and weak with frustration and hopelessness,
God is there.
Even now when you cannot see Him or feel Him,
His arms are around you.

During this darkest hour,
when you don't have the strength or the will
to hold on anymore,
God is holding on to you.

*"[God] will never leave you
nor forsake you."*   *Joshua 1:5*

*He will keep you strong to the end,
so that you will be blameless
on the day of our Lord Jesus Christ.
God,*
> *who has called you into fellowship
> with his Son Jesus Christ our Lord,*
is faithful.
> > *1 Corinthians 1:8–9*

*For I am convinced
that neither death nor life,
neither angels nor demons,
neither the present nor the future,
nor any powers,
neither height nor depth,
nor anything else in all creation
will be able to separate us
from the love of God
that is in Christ Jesus our Lord.*
> > *Romans 8:38–39*

Where is God?

Where is God?
when children die,
when mothers shake
and fathers cry,
while—stunned—they mumble,
"Jesus—*why?*"
and beat against
a frozen sky.

Where is God!
when icy age
deposes youth
and takes the stage,
becomes an enemy—
a cage,
and forces joy
to helpless rage.

The world is racked
with pain and fraud,
and we whose shoulders
once were broad
now weep
while Satan's hosts applaud
our angry insult—
Where is God?

*"How I long for the months gone by,
for the days when God
watched over me,
when his lamp shone upon my head
and by his light I walked through
darkness!
. . . I cry out to you, O God,
but you do not answer;
I stand up, but you merely look at me.
You turn on me ruthlessly;
with the might of your hand
you attack me.
You snatch me up
and drive me before the wind;
you toss me about in the storm.
I know
you will bring me
down to
death,
to the place appointed
for all the living."*
Job 29:2–3; 30:20–23

Anger

Don't *tell* me
how I'm supposed to feel!
Don't tell me I can't be angry.

I **AM** angry!

Don't turn away
or hide your eyes,
don't be afraid of me like this.
Don't patronize
or simplify
or smile nervously and look at each other.
Oh, don't reject me now!

This anger *is* me.
This is all I am right now,
all I can be.

Oh, please love me still.

*The eternal God is your refuge,
and underneath
are the everlasting arms.*
Deuteronomy 33:27

*Your love, O LORD,
reaches to the heavens,
your faithfulness to the skies.
How priceless is your unfailing love!
Both high and low among men
find refuge
in the shadow of your wings.*
Psalm 36:5,7

Why me?

Have you hurled your accusations heavenward?
Have you lodged your complaints against God?
Have you shaken your fist in the face of the Father,
or bitterly hidden your heart
from His voice?
God may seem distant now,
and your rebellion may seem justified.
But He
is sovereign.
He has all rights, all power.
He is the Potter
in a Potter's world,
and we are all
but clay.

God does not *owe* us an explanation,
but He always has a reason.
   He is not random or whimsical.
   He is not distant or casual.
   He does not make mistakes.
God is God.
The Potter in a Potter's world.

The molding may be painful.
The shaping often hurts.
We sometimes must be broken, even crushed.

But if you let Him,
He will re-make you,
and turn your clay to finest gold.

*So I went down to the potter's house,
and I saw him working at the wheel.
But the pot he was shaping from the
clay was marred in his hands;
so the potter
formed it into another pot,
shaping it as seemed best to him.*
Jeremiah 18:3–4

*The LORD said to Job:
"Will the one who contends with the
Almighty correct him? Let him who
accuses God answer him!"
Then Job answered the LORD:
I am unworthy—how can I reply to
you?… Surely I spoke
of things I did not understand,
things too wonderful for me to know."*
Job 40:1–4; 42:3

*"No eye has seen, no ear has heard,
no mind has conceived what God has
prepared for those who love him."*
1 Corinthians 2:9

*Answer me when I call to you,
O my righteous God.
Give me relief
from my distress;
be merciful to me
and hear my prayer.*
Psalm 4:1

Why pain?

The Bible paints a picture
of an involved and compassionate God.

From the very beginning,
when He stooped down
on hands and knees
in the dust and stuff of earth
to form
fashion
with His own hands
Man,
He has loved us as His children.

His commitment is so intense
so actual
that He willingly forced himself
into a human body with a specific lifespan,
and lived like us,
felt all the things we feel.

His own pain
was not somehow easier because He was God.
Nor was He stoic and passionless.
He sweated and shook and wept,
"Do I have to die?"
He screamed in agony
and cried out tearfully,
"My God! Where are you?"

This God knows pain.

Although His power
could somehow swallow suffering,
erase pain,
He chooses not to.

And *that*
we don't understand.

The mystery is
that pain is somehow essential.
It exists
not as proof
that God doesn't care,
but as a part of life
so significant
that removing it
would make us *less*.

Rather than effortlessly
banishing pain,
God has chosen to share it
intimately
with us.

See the scars on His hands?

Praying for a miracle

Do you dare
wrestle with the angel?
Do you dare struggle with God
and wrench a blessing from Him?
Is your faith
a *grappling* faith?
Does your faith
take hold?

Or are you afraid to even ask?

What does Christ's resurrection mean for us
if not actual victory?
Why
did He die
if not to give us life?
Christ's resurrection from actual, physical death
is no metaphor, no
possibility;
Christ's resurrection *happened*!

It *happens*.

Reach out and grasp
the hem of His garment—
feel His living power—
not in desperation, not in resignation,
in *faith*.

Do you dare?

Is any one of you in trouble? He should pray. Is anyone happy? Let him sing songs of praise. Is any one of you sick? He should call the elders of the church to pray over him and anoint him with oil in the name of the Lord. And the prayer offered in faith will make the sick person well; the Lord will raise him up. If he has sinned, he will be forgiven. Therefore confess your sins to each other and pray for each other so that you may be healed. The prayer of a righteous man is powerful and effective.
James 5:13–16

Just then a woman who had been subject to bleeding for twelve years came up behind him and touched the edge of his cloak. She said to herself, "If I only touch his cloak, I will be healed." Jesus turned and saw her. "Take heart, daughter," he said, "your faith has healed you." And the woman was healed from that moment.
Matthew 9:22–23

Accepting God's answer

Do you dare
accept an answer you didn't want?
Do you dare sincerely ask,
knowing He might say *no*?
Is your faith
an *open* faith?
Can your faith
let go?

Or are you closed to other possibilities?

What does God's creative power mean for us
if not complete control?
Why does He call us His children
if not to tenderly father us?
God's wisdom, His grasp of *your* situation,
is unquestionable.
His love is not dependent on the size of your faith
or the fervency of your prayers.
His love *is*!

It always *will be*.

Open your heart to the healing *God* chooses—
peace in place of bitterness,
              calm in place of fear,
                          hope in the face of death
Open your faith.
                                  Do you dare?

"Which of you, if his son asks for bread, will give him a stone? Or if he asks for a fish, will give him a snake? If you, then, though you are evil, know how to give good gifts to your children, how much more will your Father in heaven give good gifts to those who ask him!"
Matthew 7:9–11

Three times I pleaded with the Lord to take [this burden] away from me. But he said to me, "My grace is sufficient for you, for my power is made perfect in weakness." Therefore I will boast all the more gladly about my weaknesses, so that Christ's power may rest on me. That is why, for Christ's sake, I delight in weaknesses, in insults, in hardships, in persecutions, in difficulties. For when I am weak, then I am strong.
2 Corinthians 12:8–10

Lonely

Their easy chatter dances,
    laughing, near me, while
    I
    stand against the
    wall,
    trying to
    look
    comfortable.

Activity, busyness, conversation
    ring around me, skipping,
    never take
    my
    hand.
    I pretend not to mind.

I smile and nod,
    try to think of
    something
    to say,
    look normal on the outside
    just like I used to be,
    everything's okay.

But inside I'm alone

and it hurts.

These used to be my friends.

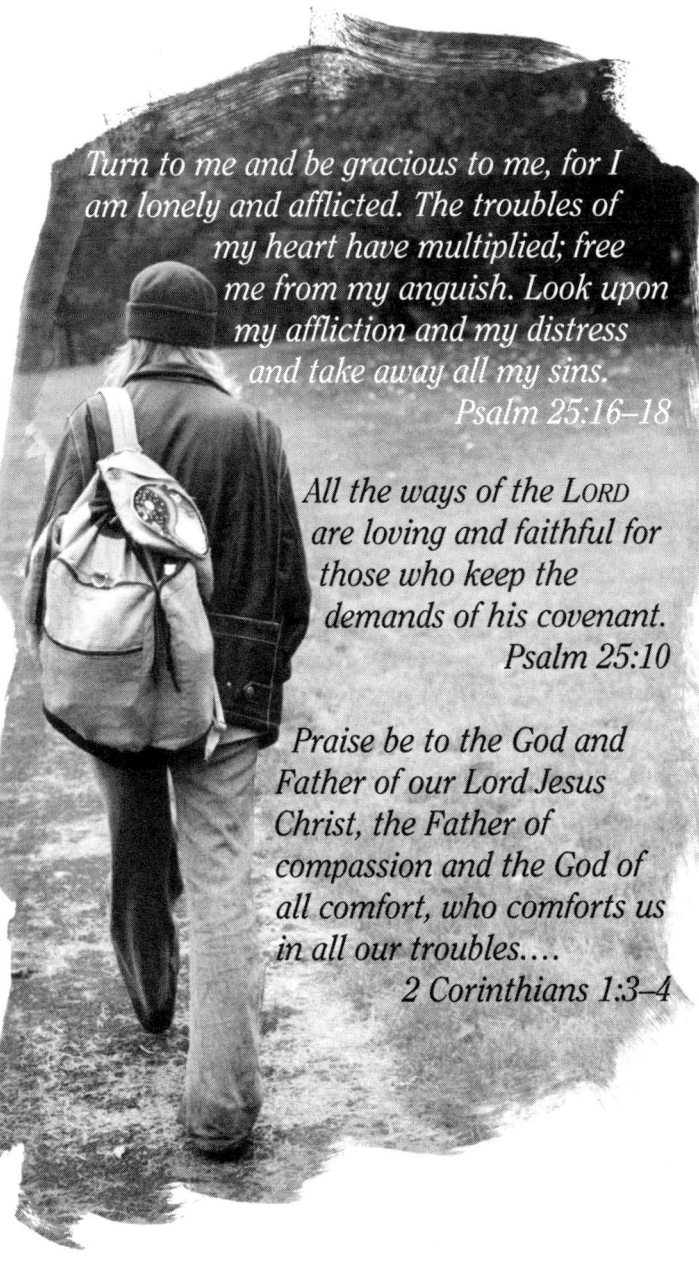

Turn to me and be gracious to me, for I am lonely and afflicted. The troubles of my heart have multiplied; free me from my anguish. Look upon my affliction and my distress and take away all my sins.
Psalm 25:16–18

All the ways of the LORD are loving and faithful for those who keep the demands of his covenant.
Psalm 25:10

Praise be to the God and Father of our Lord Jesus Christ, the Father of compassion and the God of all comfort, who comforts us in all our troubles....
2 Corinthians 1:3–4

roken

When your grief is so sharp
and your pain so tight
that it leaves you gasping
and almost crazy—

When fear and shame and flashing anger
are all exploding
in your head and chest,
and depression swarms you—

When you finally think, "This is it. This is too much!
This is more than I can bear!"
and you know your heart is straining
but you cannot let it burst—

                                            Let it burst
Let your heart break. Let go and fall apart.

Your tortured sobs reach compassionate ears,
and He whose own heart was pierced
will gently bind up yours.

With sympathetic tears and vivid understanding,
our suffering Christ holds us,
nodding, gently rocking,
until the storm is past.

And with the morning, whenever it may come,
He brings us healing peace.

*He heals the brokenhearted
and bins up their wounds.*
                               Psalm 147:3

*Cast all your anxiety on him
because he cares
for you.*
                               1 Peter 5:7

*And the peace of God, which
transcends all understanding,
will guard your hearts and your
minds in Christ Jesus.*
                               Philippians 4:7

Silence

Well-meaning visitors
chase away the silence that threatens,
with forced cheerfulness
and desperate stabs
at random topics of conversation.
Hospital staffers interrupt
with pills and linens
and one more test.
Even the pain itself sometimes
drives silence from my mind.

I am never alone with my thoughts.

With time so precious now, these banalities
frustrate me.
*I **need** silence.*
I need solitude.

Please—
    give me the time
    the silence
    the solitude
    to face my   death,
to stare at it closely—
even if it hurts—
and *meet* it
rather than be
overtaken
by it.

"Be still and know that I am God."
Psalm 46:10

There is a time for everything,
and a season
for every activity under heaven:
a time to be born and a time to die,…
a time to kill and a time to heal,
a time to tear down
and a time to build,
a time to weep and a time to laugh,
a time to mourn
and a time to dance,…
a time to be silent
> *and a time to speak.…*
Ecclesiastes 3:1–7

A light in the darkness

Any time now.

Soon.   Or maybe not.

Any breath could be your last.

Each day
each hour
each very moment
joins the countdown
while you hover.

Time vanishes
and you mourn each moment past,
until grief for those past
fills those present
and
gently
drags you under.

The blackness is thick
almost alive
deceptively comforting
convincingly strong
exhausting
heavy
deep.

But not impenetrable.

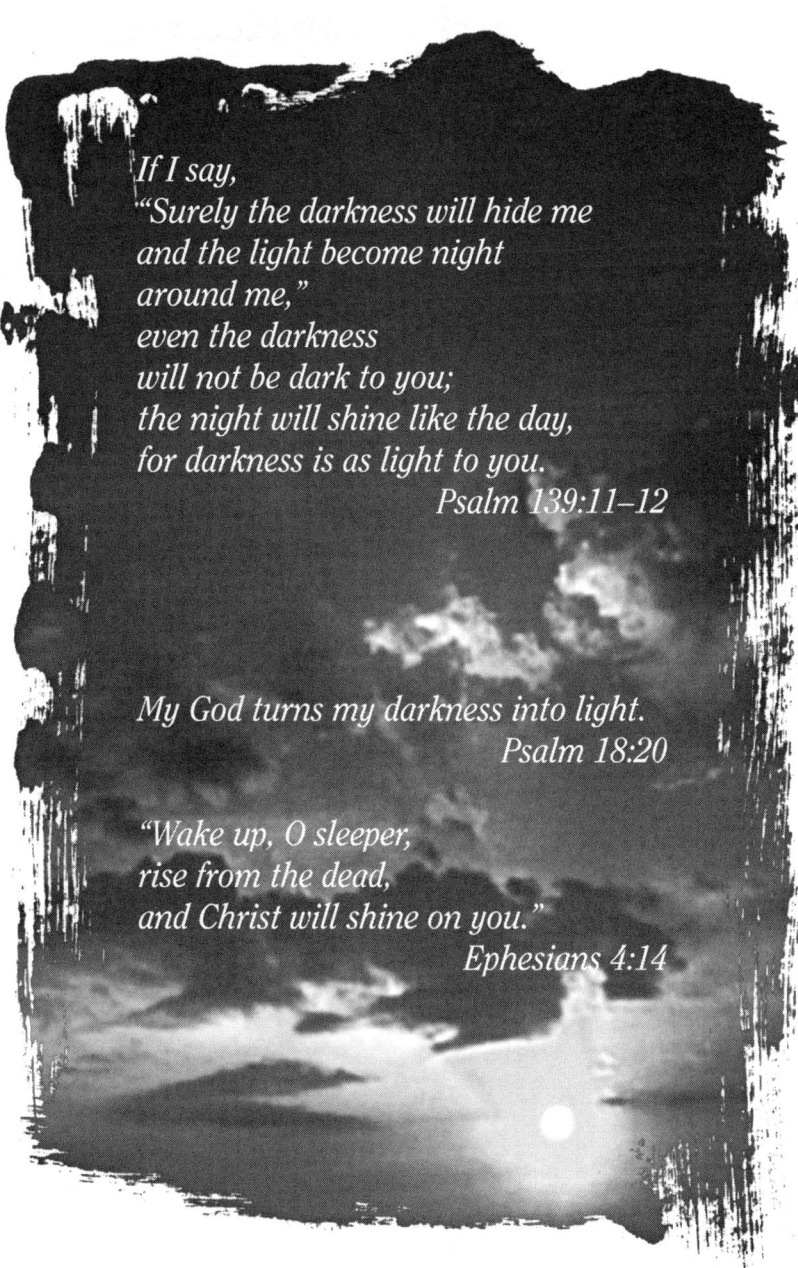

*If I say,
"Surely the darkness will hide me
and the light become night
around me,"
even the darkness
will not be dark to you;
the night will shine like the day,
for darkness is as light to you.*
  Psalm 139:11–12

My God turns my darkness into light.
  Psalm 18:20

*"Wake up, O sleeper,
rise from the dead,
and Christ will shine on you."*
  Ephesians 4:14

What good can come of this?

A river in Palestine
called the Jordan
flows into the Sea of Galilee,
rushes out again,
then empties into the Dead Sea, where it dies.

The Sea of Galilee
jumps and sparkles—
fish thrive, plants green,
birds nest.
It lives
because it gives.
It accepts the Jordan,
then releases it;
inhales, exhales,
and stays alive.

The Dead Sea
has no outlet.
The Jordan pours in
and stays,
choked.
Salt and stagnation
leave the water
barren.
Death swallows life.
The end of the line.
            Or so it seems.

Though the Dead Sea's earthly bounds
trap
the Jordan,
the river finds release:
with nowhere else to go,
it turns skyward and evaporates.

The residue it leaves
is fertile chemical,
enriching silt
that brings life to fruitless earth.

A stagnant end
to a fruitful life
may seem pointless.

The finality
and suddenness
of death
may seem to
erase
meaning
from years of giving and living.

> What *purpose* do
> painful waiting
> and narrowed options serve?
>
> *Why* do people suffer?
>
> What good can come of this?

If you can find the strength
to turn yourself heavenward,

> you can know
> that God will bring forth
>
>   hope
>
> from acid brine,
>
>   and life
>   even from death.

> *Now we see but a poor reflection as in a mirror; then we shall see face to face. Now I know in part; then I shall know fully, even as I am fully known.*
> *1 Corinthians 13:12*

Keeping the faith

Hell's prosecutor
takes the floor,
strutting,
thumbs in the lapels of his robe,
and begins to build his case:
"If a woman were struck with cancer
just a week after she had achieved her dream
of completing medical school
so she could serve the city's poor—
                                    her faith would crumble!"

And heaven's defense attorney
rises,
calls to the stand
just such a woman, whose faith was tested
in just such a way
but didn't crumble.
Evidence to the contrary.

A second scenario by the prosecution:
"Suppose a man contracted AIDS
and was deserted by his friends, his family,
his church,
and left to die alone—
                                      his faith would crumble."

Followed by the defense's second witness,
whose faith was tested in just such a way
but didn't crumble.
More evidence to the contrary.

On and on the trial goes,
Satan stomping, sweating,
filing grand accusations, drawing grand conclusions,
hour after hour,
each one different from the last.

But for each scenario a name is supplied—
more evidence to the contrary.

Each of us has a unique position
on the cosmic battleground.
Each of us is a key witness in the galactic trial.
For we each come from
a situation
a set of circumstances
a combination of factors
completely
unlike
anyone else's.
The personal, individual afflictions
we each live through today
have not been lived through by anyone else,
nor will they be again.

And our faith, then,
takes on additional significance,
for it factors into the huge heavenly drama,

as well as making us whole.

Assurance

The LORD is my shepherd,
I shall not be in want.
He makes me lie down in green pastures,
he leads me beside quiet waters,
he restores my soul.
He guides me in paths of righteousness
for his name's sake.

Even though I walk through the valley of the
shadow of death,
I will fear no evil, for you are with me;
your rod and your staff,
they comfort me.
You prepare a table before me
in the presence of my enemies.
You anoint my head with oil;
my cup overflows.

Surely goodness and love will follow me
all the days of my life,
and I will dwell
in the house of the LORD forever.

Psalm 23

Healing

I love the LORD, for he heard my voice;
he heard my cry for mercy.
Because he turned his ear to me,
I will call on him as long as I live.

The cords of death entangled me,
the anguish of the grave came upon me;
I was overcome by trouble and sorrow.
Then I called on the name of the LORD:
"O LORD, save me!"

The LORD is gracious and righteous;
our God is full of compassion.
The LORD protects the simplehearted;
when I was in great need, he saved me.

Be at rest once more, O my soul,
for the LORD has been good to you.

For you, O LORD, have delivered
my soul from death,
my eyes from tears,
my feet from stumbling,
that I may walk before the LORD
in the land of the living.

Psalm 116:1–9

Raised in glory

Think not, of course,
that this is me,
this withered shoot,
this house of clay,
this hill of dust
soon blown away;
this stagg'ring fragile child you see
is not the whole, completed me.

Death I know will set me free,
will melt my shackles,
break my chains,
release my spirit,
ease my pains,
and land me at the crystal sea.

My death will finally set me free.

So will it be with the resurrection of the dead.
The body that is sown is perishable,
it is raised imperishable;
it is sown in dishonor,
it is raised in glory;
it is sown in weakness,
it is raised in power;
it is sown a natural body,
it is raised a spiritual body.
1 Corinthians 15:42–44

Therefore we are always confident and know that as long as we are at home in the body we are away from the Lord.
2 Corinthians 5:6

But we have this treasure in jars of clay to show that this all-surpassing power is from God and not from us.
2 Corinthians 4:7

> *The dust returns to the ground it came from, and the spirit returns to God who gave it.*
> *Ecclesiastes 12:7*

Letting go

This fragile housing,
so long my prison,
now faces its destruction,
and soon will be remade, renewed.

My heart and soul
prepare to spring
from the fists of earth
to the arms of my Savior.

Living death gives way to life reborn.

Angels welcome me,
crying with joy,
and Christ Himself applauds my arrival.

Wonder becomes excitement,
then unbridled thrill,
and I race the streets of heaven,
dancing, calling out,
re-meeting those
who had left me behind for awhile.
O the wonder of it!

What made me cling to earth so long?

Then I saw a new heaven and a new earth, for the first heaven and the first earth had passed away, and there was no longer any sea. I saw the Holy City, the new Jerusalem, coming down out of heaven from God, prepared as a bride beautifully dressed for her husband. And I heard a loud voice from the throne saying, "Now the dwelling of God is with men, and he will live with them. They will be his people, and God himself will wipe every tear from their eyes. There will be no more death or mourning or crying or pain, for the old order of things has passed away."

He who was seated on the throne said, "I am making everything new!"
Revelation 21:1–5

*Be still, and know that I
am God; I will be exalted
among the nations, I will
be exalted in the earth.*
Psalm 46:10

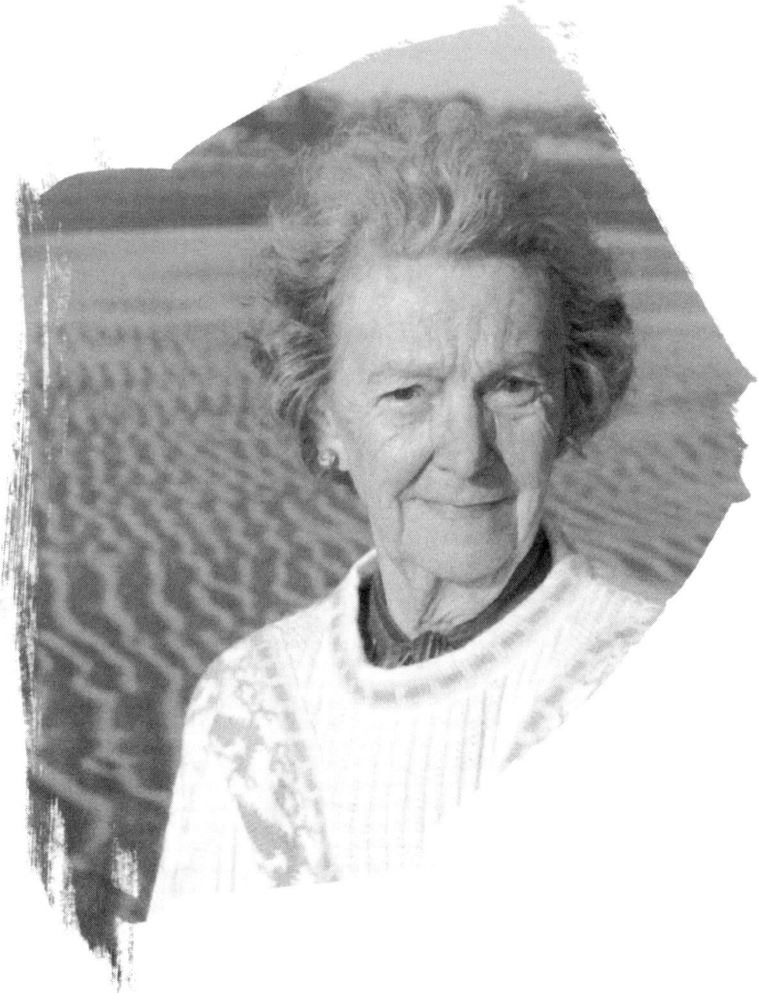

Heaven

My heaven has no passionless harp-strummers,
    no starry-eyed cloud-walkers,
    no Peter handing out wings at the gate.
Not a white-washed temple, or a misty stage,
no mass of robes and halos, no.

My heaven bristles and glows!
My Zion teems with busyness.
Its people sparkle, inside-to-out—
    stone-skippers, kite-flyers, these!

Music, yes, but not only church choirs—
    in someone's garage, guitarist and drummer
    nod laughing at each other and tap their feet.
Worship, yes,
but not only rows of saints sharing hymnbooks—
    in the studio, an artist completes a sculpture,
    and crowds applaud the Giver's gifts.

My afterlife brims—
    like the Garden of Eden—
    with fruit
    and purpose
    and God's companionship.
    It's a place prepared specifically for me
    by One whose love has never wavered.

No dream, no ghost, no drifting spirit world.
My heaven is real.

*I eagerly expect and hope that I will
in no way be ashamed, but will have
sufficient courage so that now as
always Christ will be exalted in my
body, whether by life or by death.
For to me,
to live is Christ
and to die is gain.*
Philippians 1:20–21

*Jesus said,
"I am going
to prepare a place for you.
And if I go
and prepare a place for you,
I will come back
and take you to be with me."*
John 14:2

Not the end

Even in the face of death there is hope—
because of God's promise of life

Death doesn't have to be the end.
It can be a simple transition
from this life to an even better one.

God invites you to make that transition.

Will you trust Him?

You may want to begin by telling Him
something like this:

> *Jesus, I've heard about how death was not the end for you. You faced it—and conquered it! You came back to life!*
>
> *I believe this. I believe you are alive today.*
>
> *I know I don't deserve to have you do anything for me, but I'm daring to ask: Will you save me? Will you forgive my sins? Will you help me through this?*
>
> *Will you love me no matter what? And will you help me learn to love you more?*
>
> *Thank you, Jesus. Amen.*

*Jesus said,
"I tell you the truth,
whoever hears my Word
and believes him
who sent me
has eternal life
and will not be condemned;
he has crossed over
from death to life."*
John 5:24

Want to stay close to God?

1. Read the Bible—every day!

Did you find solace in the Bible verses in this booklet? The Bible was written *by* God *for* you. Turn to it every day for comfort, assurance, and instruction. If you do not have the strength to read, ask someone to read to you, or listen to the Bible on cassette.

2. Talk to God—every day.

God wants to talk to you (when you read the Bible); and He wants to listen to you (when you pray). Praying is not as hard as you might think. Just tell God what's on your mind.

3. Keep it up.

There will be days when you don't want to read the Bible or pray—because you're weary, because you're angry with God, because it's a "bad" day, whatever. But it's worth the effort to continue—or begin—a relationship with God.

4. Let others know.

Sometimes it's not until we're face-to-face with death that we realize what life is all about—relationships. The people close to you can learn from your struggles and victories. Tell them what you're thinking about and praying about. Share how you are connecting with God and how it's helping you. Don't wait until it's too late.